PROJECT ECO-CITY

TOWN LIFE

PHILIP PARKER

Wayland

PROJECT ECO-CITY

Your Living Home
Your Wild Neighbourhood
Town Life
Global Cities

This book was prepared for Wayland (Publishers) Ltd by
Globe Education, Nantwich, Cheshire

Concept design and artwork by SPL Design

Cover picture: Feral pigeon

First published in 1994 by
Wayland (Publishers) Ltd
61 Western Road, Hove
East Sussex, BN 3 1JD, England

Printed and bound by
G. Canale & C. S. p. A., Turin

British Library Cataloguing in Publication Data
Parker Philip
Town Life. – (Project Eco-city series)
I. Title II. Series
574.5268

ISBN 0 7502 1306 X

Picture acknowledgements
Aerofilms 32
Bruce Coleman *cover* (Dr Frieder Sauer), 41 (Jane Burton)
Ecoscene 4t, 5tl (Anthony Cooper), 8t, 11b, 12 (Sally Morgan), 13 (David Purslow), 14l (Sally Morgan), 14r,
15t (Sally Morgan), 15bl (Sally Morgan), 15br (David Purslow), 19t (Sally Morgan), 19b (Anthony Cooper), 21t, 23,
24t (Sally Morgan), 27l, 29r (Nick Hawkes), 31, 33, 37l, 37r (John Farmer), 43 (Ian Harwood), 44
Heather Angel 25l
Mary Evans 6
Science Photo Library 22l (Dr Jeremy Burgess), 25rt (Dr Jeremy Burgess), 25rm (Claude Nuridsany & Marie Perennou),
25rb (Dr Jeremy Burgess)
Tesco Creative Services 11t
Tony Stone 8b (Tony Craddock), 28t (Donovan Reese)
Zefa 4b, 5tr, 5bl, 5br (J. Pfaff), 7t, 7b, 9t (E. Streichan), 9m, 9b, 10, 18, 20, 21b, 22r, 24b, 26, 27r (G. Heilman), 28b, 29l,
30 (E. Streichan), 38, 40

Contents

Towns in total

Imagine climbing up to the top of the tallest building in your town or a hill overlooking your city. What do you see? Can you see what materials your city is built from? Can you see the source of your tap water? How does electricity reach your home, and food reach the shops? Where does all the waste water and garbage go?

Like a tree or a bird – or yourself – a town takes in energy and materials from the environment (its surroundings). It changes the energy and materials and returns them as waste back to the environment.

If you think of nature in your city you may think of trees, birds, bees, squirrels and many other living things. You may think of weeds growing between the cracks in concrete. But the concrete itself is part of nature, and very much part of the city. The materials with which the city is built have been dug from the land and mountains. Forests were cut to create telephone poles, doors and furniture. Now imagine the thousands of people in your town. Add sunlight, rain, air and you have an 'ecosystem' – a group of plants and animals living together in their environment.

▲ A casualty of town life – acid rain damage to a German cathedral.

Up to one-third of a town is occupied by cars – roads, garages and parking lots.

Old buildings, modern buildings, and nature —
side-by-side in downtown Sydney, Australia.

▲ An old wood preserved
on the outskirts of a town.

▼ Sorting the rubbish for recycling
is everyday work in many towns.

Ecology is the study of how living things
affect, and are affected by, their environment.
This book is about the ecology of the whole
city – about the things that can be seen when
we look at the town in total. It is about looking
at your town as if it was a living thing that
breathes, feeds, drinks and creates wastes that
have to be removed. Your town grew to the
size it is today by doing these things.

The castle in Conwy, Wales, was built from local
stone quarried nearby.

Town origins

The history of your town is written in its buildings, hills, valleys and waterways as well as in books.

Look on a detailed map of your town for streams, rivers and old woodland. How did the people who first settled here find food, water and shelter in what is now your town? Why did they choose this particular area to settle?

Most towns and cities have grown up in places which are fairly easy to reach and have good supplies of water and food. Many towns were first built beside rivers or on natural harbours by the sea, which made it easy to move things in and out the city by boat.

An important place to site a town was where a bridge could be built across a river. Other towns were built on hills which could easily be defended and sometimes towns grew up around forts or castles.

Another important position for a town is where two or more main roads meet. In the past, such a point would have been important because people from different places could meet and buy and sell goods. 'Market towns' grew at these places.

In the last 200 years the development of industry has led to the creation and growth of many towns and cities throughout Europe and North America.

At first, these new towns were built near to where the raw materials for industry such as iron and coal were found. More recently, some new towns have been built around large cities to provide homes for city workers. Other new towns have been built in older industrial areas to attract people and new businesses from over-crowded cities.

A bird's eye view of New York city in 1855.

▲ The Australian city of Sydney grew up around a beautiful river estuary which made a fine harbour for cargo ships trading around the world.

DID YOU KNOW?

What's in a name?

The name of a town sometimes gives a clue as to why it was built. Some towns are named after a person who owned the land or built the town. Other cities have names similar to the river they were built near, or contain the words 'bridge' or 'ford' (meaning stream). The names of the UK towns, Coalville and Ironbridge, give clues as to why they grew in the early years of the Industrial Revolution.

In Europe, towns sometimes grew up around castles which provided protection.

Rock city

Look at the buildings along your street. What are they made from? Stone used for buildings comes from the ground. Look at the building materials used in your town. How many types of rock can you spot?

There are three groups of rock known as sedimentary, igneous and metamorphic. Sandstone is a sedimentary rock. It was made by the natural cementing together of tiny grains of sand over millions of years. Limestone is another sedimentary rock, and most of it was created from the crushed skeletons of creatures which lived in the sea millions of years ago. Concrete is made from a mixture of limestone and sand. Bricks are a very common building material – these are made from clay which is pressed into a rectangular shape and baked in an oven. Clay is also a sedimentary material.

Deep underground, rocks are very hot. At a depth of just 6 km, the temperature is twice as hot as boiling water. But hundreds of kilometres below the surface it can be hot enough for the rock to melt. Igneous rocks are created when this molten material cools into a solid. As it cools, shiny minerals form within. Granite is an igneous rock and old buildings in Aberdeen, Scotland, are made of the local dark granite.

▲ Concrete is a modern, manufactured building material.

▼ In earlier times, natural stone was used for important buildings as seen here in Copenhagen.

Some big buildings have beautiful, shiny marble walls or floors. Marble is a metamorphic rock – it was created when rocks were heated up and squashed by the weight of rocks above. The marble you see in a building may have been carved from a mountain thousands of kilometres away. Slate is another metamorphic rock. In mid-Wales, many roofs are built from this dark material which is quarried nearby.

▲ Plastic and glass in a Parisian business district – materials that have their origins in nature.

◄ The Supreme Court, Washington DC. Beautiful marble floors and columns provide a fitting environment for the most important legal events in the USA.

The roofs of the buildings in this Welsh town are made from the slate quarried from the surrounding hills.

Urban heritage

Just as a town's name can sometimes suggest why it was built, street names often give clues about different parts of the city. Some names suggest which parts of the city were built first and which of the buildings are the oldest. Other names give clues as to who lived in the street, who built it, and which streets were the most important for which activities. 'Telegraph Hill' and 'Spring Street' are examples from the US city San Francisco, which also has an old area called 'Fisherman's Wharf'.

How many different kinds of architecture are there in your town? Are there any very old timber-framed buildings, or some even older? How old is the oldest church or cathedral? Does your town have many modern buildings covered in steel and glass? Sometimes buildings with very different styles exist side by side. This can make an exciting contrast, but not always. Which buildings do you like? Why do you think it is important to preserve attractive buildings from former times?

A well-known view of Manhattan, New York City. For many years the 1931 Empire State building was the tallest building in the world.

Chrysler Building

Empire State Building

The history of a town is written in its buildings. As the town changes, the needs of the buildings change too. As new industries replace old, buildings, wharfs and mills become empty. Once people lived in the centre of a town, but as it grows many people move to the suburbs. The houses they leave behind often become shops. Even churches, hospitals and railway stations have been abandoned – and later used as shops or theatres. Sometimes these buildings have rare and interesting features.

This 1930s building in the UK is protected by law as a fine example of the style of the time – once a factory it is now a supermarket.

An old church may have statues, or a 150 year old building may be unchanged from when it was first built. The law can stop these buildings from being demolished. In the UK such buildings are 'listed' and their original style of architecture can be protected.

DID YOU KNOW?

History along the river bank

Rivers can show a lot about the history of the town. Plants along the river's edge were used by early industries. The leaves of soapwort make a lather which was used as a cleaner in cloth mills. If this plant is found today growing by the side of rivers and streams it may show the site of an old wash-house or mill. Teasel was also used in mills where its rough seeds were used to brush newly-woven cloth. Willow was often grown: the bark contains asprin – a cure for headaches.

An ancient statue on Magdeburg Cathedral, Germany.

Town woodland

Old woodlands, rivers and streams can be among the most important wildlife habitats in towns.

Are there any clues around to tell you what grew in your area before your town was built? Is there any old woodland, or 'trapped' remains of woods or meadows in a churchyard? Surprisingly, one of the biggest examples of original woodland in New York state, USA, is a group of hemlock trees in the Botanical Gardens in the heart of New York City!

For thousands of years much of northern Europe and parts of North America were covered in forest. In these regions, almost every village and town began as a clearing in the woodland. Over the centuries, the forests were cut down for building materials and to burn as the settlements grew in size. In the twentieth century, this loss has accelerated – the UK has lost half its old woodland in the last 50 years. The small 'pockets' of woodland that remain are also under threat from plans to build more houses, roads, reservoirs and factories.

Town woods are very important habitats. Just one oak tree can act as food or shelter for 68 species of bird, 34 species of butterfly, 271 species of other insects and 32 species of mammal from field mice to weasels. Wildflowers are also protected by the shade of a tree. A town wood is like a small island within a city.

Thousands of New York's trees are concentrated in its Central Park in Manhattan.

New forests are important. In the UK, the government is working with local groups to create a dozen 'community forests' on the edges of major cities. These will be on empty derelict ground and provide a large area of green for town dwellers to enjoy. The American Forestry Association plans to plant 400 million trees in urban areas of the USA.

In central town, tawny owls mostly eat birds. In woods on the outskirts, mammals may be 90 per cent of their diet.

PLANT A TREE

Choose a site to plant your tree. If you plant it on your birthday you can compare your height with the tree's growth each year.

A tree from a seed
Collect freshly-fallen seeds in autumn, especially acorns or beech nuts. Sow them in pots filled with moist compost. In spring, they may begin to grow. It could take a year for a seedling to grow to a height of 10 cm when it will be ready to plant outdoors. Find a sheltered place and dig a hole the size of your pot. Remove the plant and compost and put in the hole. Keep it well watered.

Planting a tree seedling.

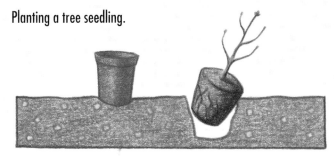

A tree from a garden centre
Buy the tree in spring. Check that the roots are strong and cover them in a black bag to keep them moist. Dig a hole deep enough for the roots and break up the soil at the bottom of the hole with a fork. Place the tree carefully in the hole and pack soil around the roots. Firm the soil down gently with your foot and water generously. Pour on about 15-20 litres a day for a month, then 2 or 3 times a week until midsummer. Keep the soil at its base free from grass and weeds.

Planting a young tree.

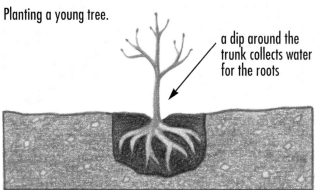

a dip around the trunk collects water for the roots

Wild waters

Rivers can be the richest of all town habitats. But where does all the water come from? Rain or snow falls into a 'catchment area' – land that provides a river with water. Water trickles down through soil and rock and eventually emerges as a spring or stream which leads into a river. Other streams feed the river and a fast-flowing body of water builds up. Towns add greatly to this water flow as the river passes through. Rainwater drains from roofs and streets straight into gutters and drains which channel the water into the river as well as sewers.

A town river has several different habitats for wildlife to flourish. With a strong current sweeping in one direction, plants must be anchored to the river bed. These plants usually have underwater leaves, but in slow-moving rivers plants with floating leaves grow. Insect larvae have strong claws to grasp rocks and plants; their smooth, flat bodies are streamlined to ensure the minimum of drag on them by the water.

Scientists are no longer sure what species of fish originally swam in industrial towns. Pollution during the Industrial Revolution killed most groups of fish during the last 200 years, and today's groups are different.

Sticklebacks can survive in water that is slightly polluted.

A typical town river with pondweed thriving.

As rivers slowly become cleaner, eels and stickleback return, followed by perch, pike and minnow, and eventually trout and salmon.

On the river bank, one or two species of fast-growing weed may dominate and scattered trees and shrubs may grow. Patches of woodland or scrub near the river are home to bird species who use the river for food. Other species live in the river. Mallard and moorhen are very common. Their success in breeding depends on how often the river floods their nests and on how many rats there are to take eggs and young birds. Kingfishers have adapted to town rivers, sometimes nesting in disused pipes alongside the banks, and fishing for minnows and sticklebacks. In the winter many more bird species use the river for feeding and resting.

Monkey flower may well have been accidentally brought to British canals on ships from the USA.

◄ A town river contains many habitats: moving water, the river bottom and edge, weeds and woods.

As the amounts of pollution in many of our town rivers fall, so kingfishers are returning to built-up areas.

15

Clean rivers?

As a river passes through a town, a wide range of materials enter it, including sewage. This is the waste water from homes and factories. It is usually treated to remove decaying materials, but sometimes only partially-treated sewage reaches a river. Bacteria and simple plants feed on the decaying material and use up the oxygen dissolved in the river water. All living things, except certain bacteria, need oxygen to survive. Some creatures need more oxygen than others.

The larvae of both the mayfly and the stonefly need a lot of oxygen and are not usually found in town rivers. If there are no freshwater shrimps which need plenty of oxygen then your river is probably slightly polluted. Many industries and power stations empty hot waste water into rivers. Hot water holds less oxygen than cold and downstream from a waste pipe the numbers of these sensitive shrimps is usually far less.

Leeches are related to earthworms and have segmented bodies, but unlike earthworms also have suckers. Most leeches feed by attaching themselves to a fish or snail and sucking the blood. Since blood contains oxygen, leeches can survive in fairly polluted water.

Pollution indicator

Scientists can measure the amount of oxygen in water in a laboratory. There is a quicker way to find out how polluted a river is. Some species of animals can live with a lot of pollution; others are very sensitive to it. By looking at which species are missing in a river, we can find out how clean it is.

freshwater shrimp

leech

hog louse

rat-tailed maggot
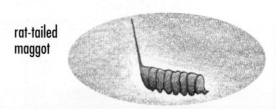

clean

slightly polluted

fairly polluted

badly polluted

mayfly
nymph

stonefly nymph

Very polluted water will have hog lice which are relatives of woodlice. Any stone, piece of wood or rubbish pulled out will probably be crawling with them. The worst polluted rivers are covered in a brown or yellow slime of bacteria and simple plant life. In this horrible mass only the very pollution-resistant creatures such as the tubifex worm and the rat-tailed maggot can live. The rat-tailed maggot does not attempt to draw oxygen from the water – it has a long tube which rises above the water to draw in oxygen from the air, rather like a diver with a snorkel.

HOW CLEAN IS YOUR RIVER?

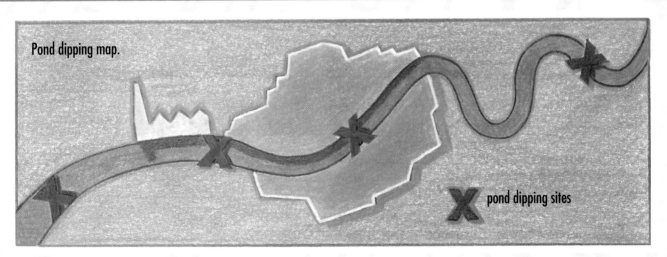

Pond dipping map.

X pond dipping sites

Don't be deceived – polluted water often looks clean and clear if there is not much life in it.

Use a small net to sweep gently through the water near the bank. Lift stones and sweep around them. Empty the net into a tray which has a little water in it. Use a magnifying glass to identify your catch and make drawings of it.

Repeat the sweep to see what other life there is and compare your findings with the chart (opposite) to find how clean the water is.

Repeat the test again at different places on the river – before a built-up part or a factory, and after it, for example.

For safety, always take an adult with you when you are working near a river.

Turning the tide

As well as sewage, rivers are used as dumps for a huge range of materials. In the UK a three-year study by 1,600 children looked at 60 rivers. They found that rivers are used to dump everything from drinks cans to cars.

Less obvious is the chemical pollution of rivers by some industries and farms. The bottom of New York's Hudson River, for example, is lined with a poisonous sludge. Years of dumping of chemicals by industries have left dangerous wastes that all but killed the river, reducing it to a brown, foul smelling eye-sore from above the state capital, Albany, down to New York City.

Almost 30 years ago, local people came together to patrol the Hudson and find companies dumping illegal waste.
This group grew to more than 10,000 people achieving many successes in preventing the dumping of forbidden materials and organizing the removal of poisonous sludge from stretches of the river.

In Europe, keeping rivers clean is more difficult since the rivers pass through two or more countries on their way to the sea – and sometimes countries don't co-operate over reducing pollution.

The 510 km long River Hudson flows to the Atlantic Ocean at New York city.

In November 1986, a fire at a chemical company by the Rhine in Switzerland released a massive spill of chemicals which killed at least 500,000 fish. For a whole day, Switzerland did not tell the three nations downstream about the spill.

In most countries, laws have been passed under which industries need special permission to release waste into rivers. Pollution of rivers by sewage and industry has been reduced in the last 20 years, but it has been much harder to control chemicals washed into rivers from farmland.

The Rhine – Europe's most polluted river.

REBIRTH OF THE RIVER THAMES

In the early 1800s, fishermen could still catch thousands of salmon a year from the Thames near London. But Thames salmon were sold for a high price in the local markets – a sign that they were becoming rare – and the last salmon was caught in the 1830s. Pollution from sewers and industry flowing directly into the river was wiping out all the wildlife. By the 1950s, the lower 70 km of the Thames was almost without fish. New sewage treatment plants were built and within ten years more than 40 species of fish had returned. By 1975 there were around 85 different species. The rising numbers of fish also attracted dozens of species of water birds. Salmon were seen once more in the 1980s and today more than 150 species of fish thrive in the river. Although during hot weather algae can grow in large numbers, a boat called the 'Thames Bubbler' is on hand if the oxygen in the river gets too low. It has pipes which can bubble oxygen into the water.

The Thames Bubbler is equipped with a pump to bubble oxygen into London's river should the oxygen level in the water fall dangerously low.

Heat islands

As the air above a city is warmed it rises up into the sky. The space it leaves behind draws in fresh air from the countryside. The city 'breathes in' – and it also 'breathes out' waste gases.

The spring arrives early in northern cities in Europe and America. Plants blossom into life several weeks earlier than the same species in the countryside. In the autumn, very cold weather and frosts come later. City plants can have up to 10 weeks more growing time than country plants. And the animals that feed and shelter in those plants also have more time to grow and breed. This is because towns are usually warmer than the surrounding countryside.

The concrete and asphalt of a city are heated by the sun during the day and they store some of this heat. In the countryside the sun's energy is mostly reflected. At night, the city surfaces release the heat so that city centres can be 5 °C warmer than the countryside around them. By dawn, the heat stored in the material of the buildings and roads has been released – only to increase again during the day. A 'heat island' builds up over the city.

A new day dawns in Hong Kong – the sun is beginning to heat the city and a heat island starts to develop.

The heat island creates a flow of air into and out of the city. Warm air over the city rises and slowly floats out to the cooler countryside. The air then cools down and falls, where it will be pulled back towards the city to replace the rising warm air.

Cities are also warmer because of the heat generated by machinery in factories and by vehicles. Heating and air-conditioning systems in homes and offices also give out heat. As well as being warmer, scientists have found that cities are also less windy, cloudier and up to 10 per cent wetter than the country. The sudden downpours and storms can overload a town's drains and sewage can flow into streams and rivers.

▲ A cherry tree blossoming in town weeks before cherry trees in the country.

A summer rainstorm in Paris – a pedestrian shelters beneath an umbrella.

DID YOU KNOW?

Windy cities

On average, winds are up to 20 per cent slower in cities because they drag around the buildings. But high buildings also 'squeeze' the wind, speeding it up. Australia's windiest city is Perth where the buildings channel strong winds down to the street. Miniature whirlpools can be created at the base of buildings, making them uncomfortable places to be around. The circling movement of leaves and litter in the street near buildings shows this effect.

Fit to breathe

The air that is warmed and rises above a city carries with it tiny particles of soot and dust. Cooler air is drawn into the city centre over the suburbs where it can collect more dust and pollution. This is one reason why the centre is more polluted than other parts of the city. The dust and pollution-filled air can be held in place by a layer of cold air above. Cities that are surrounded by hills, such as Los Angeles, or are built in a valley can suffer from this. The pollution is trapped over the city, like soup in a bowl, and can combine with the moisture in the air to form smogs.

▲ Car pollution in particular is responsible for Los Angeles' smogs.

◄ A magnified view of a grain of grass pollen which can cause hay fever. Air pollution may be making city people more sensitive to pollen.

Mexico City has one of the worst air pollution records in the world. It is believed that 90 per cent of the breathing problems of people living there come from air pollution. In richer countries, too, allergies and breathing problems from asthma to hay fever are on the increase in cities. Scientists are beginning to believe that some of the chemicals from car, bus and lorry exhausts are causing allergies and leading to the increase in asthma.

As well as gases, the particles from vehicle exhausts are thought to be causing serious health problems. These tiny particles are so small they can be breathed in right to the furthest parts of human lungs – taking damaging chemicals with them. The result could be lung and heart diseases. A US scientist has calculated that perhaps 60,000 people a year die in the USA due to this kind of pollution. In UK cities, up to 10,000 people could be dying every year – all because of the unfit air.

A machine checking the sulphur pollution of city air in Czechoslovakia.

INVESTIGATING AIR POLLUTION

The best leaves to test for pollution are those on trees and bushes which don't lose their leaves in winter.

Select a leaf at about your height and carefully dip it in the jar half-filled with water. Use the paintbrush to wash both its sides. Repeat this with nine other nearby leaves. Now pour the dirty water through some filter paper into another jar. Remove the filter paper and let it dry – the dirt from the leaves will be on the paper.

Testing for air pollution.

wash off 10 leaves into a jam jar

filter the wash water then let the filter paper dry

keep a record of your test sites

Repeat this test on similar-sized leaves in different places. Compare your results and make a 'pollution map' of the area showing which areas had most pollution, and which had little.

Life with pollution

The effects of pollution in cities can often be seen in dirty, sooty walls and trees, and even in the damage to buildings by 'acid rain' caused by air pollution. Living things are also affected by pollution. The most sensitive species die or move away, leaving fewer but hardier species behind. Some species even benefit from changes brought by pollution.

A good example of a species coping with pollution is the peppered moth. Pollution affects trees in two ways – it kills lichens growing on them and a layer of soot can coat the bark leaving a darker tree. The peppered moth has its name because it has white wings with a speckling of black. In 1848 a black variety was seen in the UK industrial city of Manchester. Fifty years later almost all peppered moths here were black. The same was found in other industrial cities, but the white variety was still the most common in country areas. The reason for this is that on the blackened trees, the black moths could not be seen by birds. But the white ones could easily be detected and eaten. In this way, more black moths survived than white, and so more black moths could breed.

▲ Acid rain caused by air pollution is rotting the stone of this old English cathedral.

Plane trees can tolerate air pollution. Their bark peels off and keeps the breathing holes open.

Around 100 other moth species are believed to have undergone similar changes in living in dirty cities. Such changes are rare in creatures other than insects. The zebra spider is an exception. It is normally marked with black and white stripes, but in industrial areas this variety has been replaced by a wholly black one, so it is invisible on dirty trees and walls.

Peppered moths on a lichen-covered tree. One moth is the darker type which has adapted to pollution.

LOOK FOR LICHENS

There are three main types of lichens. The shrubby type looks like a leafless miniature grey-green bush 2 or 3 cm high. This species will not live in polluted air. The leafy type of lichen is less bushy, grey-green in colour, and will live in slightly polluted air. The crusty lichen grows tightly attached to the surface below it. It can look like green, orange or white paint splashes and can tolerate some pollution.

Look for lichens on walls, rocks and trees in different parts of your town. Start at the town centre and work your way out to the suburbs, looking for lichens every 0·5 km. Assess the quality of your town's air by marking on a map where you find lichens, how frequently they occur, and the different types you may find.

Shrubby lichen

Leafy lichen

Crusty lichen

Feeding the city

Inside this truck is a huge refrigerator to keep food fresh on the long journey from country to town.

Cities are hungry creatures! They consume vast amounts of food and building materials. But where does this sustenance come from?

Can you work out how many breakfasts, lunches, dinners and snacks are eaten in your town each day? If every person in a city eats three meals a day, even a medium-sized city of 100,000 people will munch almost 110 million meals in a year.

About 150 years ago in the countries that were becoming industrial, most people still grew much of their own food. Even in cities, vegetables were grown and fish, cows and chickens kept in backyards and small farms which were taken straight to the town's market. As cities grew, these areas were built over and city people became more reliant on the country for food. New ways of packaging and treating food so it could last longer were invented. The tin can, for example, allowed cooked meat, fruit and vegetables to be kept for a long time. Foods could be taken to cities by train in large quantities; stores could buy (and keep) them cheaply in bulk.

As cities become more built-up, the space available to grow food becomes less, as in Jakata, Indonesia.

Rows of battery hens laying eggs for town breakfasts.

Energy is used to create the food we take for granted. To get the most food from the land fertilizers, sprays, machinery and water are used and energy is needed to provide each. The harvesting, processing and transport to city supermarkets also need a lot of energy. With this modern intensive farming, more energy is put into the creation of food than is contained in the food we buy. Intensive farming can also lead to pollution. Fertilizers and pesticide sprays can wash into rivers and lakes which eventually end up in the city's drinking water.

DID YOU KNOW?

Your daily bread

A loaf of bread is made up of around 20 slices. They are full of energy. Growing the wheat to make the bread used the same energy as contained in 8 slices. Grinding the wheat to flour used the same energy as another 5 slices. The energy needed to bake the loaf was equal to 26 slices. One more slice of energy was needed to transport the loaf to the shop. It takes the energy of 40 slices of bread to make each 20-sliced loaf!

The rock eater!

As a city grows it needs more farmland to be worked harder to feed its body of people. It also needs materials to create its growing skeleton: buildings, roads, railways, airports and pipelines. Things like metal and wood can be brought long distances. Clay, sand, gravel and rock are bulkier and more expensive to transport, so most cities have developed a series of pits, quarries and brickworks around them. Often a reason for a city being built in a particular place was because of locally-available building materials such as clay.

Almost every town has some building work going on.

Building roads uses up land, resources and energy.

Huge quantities of gravel and rock are taken from the ground to build both cities and the roads between them. In the USA, sand and gravel pits account for a quarter of all the land disturbed by mining on the surface. These use up potential farmland to feed the city, but they can also threaten important sites for wild plants and animals. Old quarries and pits are like giant, ugly scars on the land, and they are often filled in with rubbish taken from the city. Others are turned into lakes and reservoirs. Ruxley Gravel Pits provided nearby London with building materials for 30 years before it was flooded in the 1950s and native trees planted. It is now a rare and important 'Site of Special Scientific Interest'. Many water birds, kingfishers and rare mammals such as water voles now thrive here.

This gravel pit has been flooded to create a fishing lake.

Think of all the wooden floors, furniture, fences, window frames, doors and telephone poles in your town. Now imagine the forests of trees that were cut down to make these. Almost everything in the city comes from nature. Timber is shipped to cities from around the world. Wood from distant countries can be cheaper and more readily-available than timber from your own country. Cities' demands for wood from tropical countries contribute to the destruction of the world's rainforests.

A glimpse of the pipes running under New Yorkers' feet.

THIRSTY TOWN

The energy drinker

Under the pavements of your town lies a maze of cables and pipes to feed the city's thirst for energy and water.

Cities are responsible for most of the world's energy use. Electricity provides light and power for TVs, refrigerators, machinery in factories and computers in offices. It can also heat and cool our homes and drive trains and subways. Most cities' electricity comes from the burning of 'fossil fuels'. These were formed from the bodies of ancient animal and plant life.

Over millions of years their remains were crushed and heated deep in the Earth's crust to form coal, oil and natural gas. Today, cities are burning these fossil fuels about a million times faster than they are being created in the Earth.

Some 60 per cent of the world's electricity comes from fossil fuels. Coal, oil or gas is burned in a power station and the heat boils water. The steam pushes against the blades of a turbine which drives a generator to create electricity.

In a coal-burning power station only about 35 per cent of the energy in the coal is turned into electricity. Most of the rest is lost as heat through the cooling towers.

The Torness nuclear power station on the Scottish coast.

nuclear power. A nuclear plant is rather like a fossil fuel station, but instead of burning fuels it harnesses the energy stored inside atoms. A lot of energy is created by nuclear plants, but many people fear that they are both very expensive to build and dangerous. Scientists have so far invented no safe way to store some of the hazardous nuclear waste that is created.

The electricity eventually passes through long 'transmission lines' to towns where smaller cables under the streets enter buildings. It is usual for two-thirds of the energy in the fuel to be lost in converting it to electricity and distributing it in towns.

Falling water can also be used to turn a turbine – 'hydroelectric' power stations make 20 per cent of the world's electricity. Some 15 per cent of electricity comes from

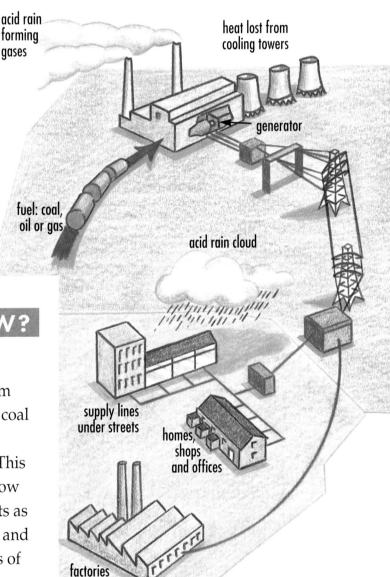

acid rain forming gases

heat lost from cooling towers

generator

fuel: coal, oil or gas

acid rain cloud

supply lines under streets

homes, shops and offices

factories

From fossil fuels to electricity in the town.

DID YOU KNOW?

King coal

Almost half the world's electricity comes from burning coal, which contains sulphur. When coal is burned, the sulphur is released and mixes with the moisture in the air to form an acid. This can fall to the ground as acid rain, mist or snow and can damage lakes, rivers, soils and forests as well as rot buildings. Many places in Europe and North America have rainfall that is hundreds of times more acid than is usual.

City waterscapes

Water is the most essential ingredient to keep cities 'alive'. It is needed for so much; not just for the citizens to drink. A power station can use 230 million litres of water every hour; making just one bag of cement needs 180 litres. Making a page of this book needed 0·5 litres of water.

Most of the largest cities draw their water from rivers and lakes. In dry weather a city could easily run short of water and many cities have built dams and reservoirs – the largest expanse of water to be found in or near a town. In the early 1900s it was found that several species of duck and gull were spending the winters on New York's new reservoirs, including many rare species.

It was so unusual to see so many species that scientists and reporters from newspapers rushed to the reservoirs to catch sight of them.

Since those days, more reservoirs have been built, and many more water birds have been attracted to them, partly because their natural wetlands were also being destroyed and drained as the cities expanded. The great crested grebe is one success story for UK reservoirs. Early this century the numbers of this bird were falling – one main reason is that their feathers were in demand to decorate hats. The increase in reservoirs allowed them to rebuild their numbers – and thankfully hat fashions changed!

Many reservoirs on the outskirts of London supply drinking water to the people living in and around the city. In winter, the reservoirs also provide a home for around 100,000 gulls.

As well as obtaining water from under the ground, California, USA, pipes in water from distant lakes and rivers along aqueducts.

Many cities and towns have rivers and lakes too small for their needs. These places take water from under the ground. Rain that soaks into the ground fills the spaces between grains of sand and in cracks and holes in rock. The water collects above a layer of waterproof rock. By drilling down into the water and pumping it up, cities can get their water supply. This 'groundwater' is the only source of drinking water for half the US population.

DID YOU KNOW?

Niagara flows

Niagara Falls on the US-Canada border carries 70,000 million litres of water over the brink each day. It would take this massive flow 17 days to fill up the 21 main reservoirs that New York City relies on – 1,200,000 million litres. New York also gets water direct from rivers. The West Delaware Tunnel brings water from the Delaware river to the city and is 170 km long making it the world's longest tunnel.

Water to drink

Until reservoirs were built, people in cities got their water from all kinds of sources. Most was taken straight from the rivers which were often highly polluted. In the early 1800s many New Yorkers depended on rainwater collected from roofs and gutters.

Today, people want water that is fit to drink: clear and clean. Water from reservoirs, rivers, or the ground is piped to a treatment plant. The US city of Chicago's main water plant is the largest in the world. It serves 4·5 million people by producing 6,600 million litres of water a day.

Chemicals are first added to the 'raw' water which collect bacteria and particles of mud. The water goes on to 'settling tanks' where the chemicals, bacteria and mud fall to the bottom and can be removed.

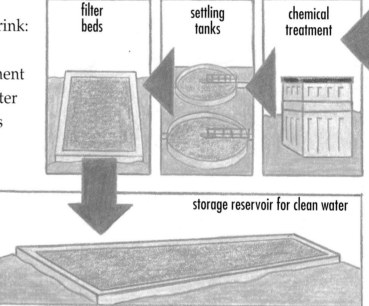

filter beds

settling tanks

chemical treatment

How drinking water reaches your town.

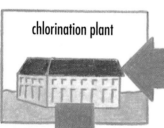

chlorination plant

storage reservoir for clean water

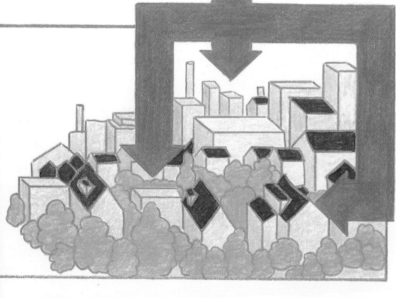

The water then trickles over a bed of sand on top of gravel. As the water seeps down it is cleaned by this filter. The water then flows to a reservoir for disinfection; chlorine is usually added to kill any remaining germs. The water can be sprayed through the air so oxygen is mixed into it – to give it a fresh smell. Further chemicals can be added to the water such as lime to stop water pipes rusting, and fluoride to help reduce tooth decay in its drinkers.

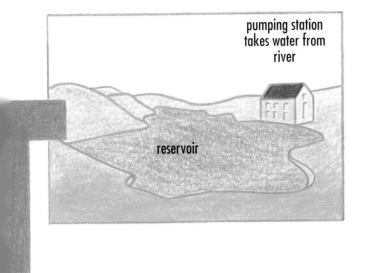

pumping station takes water from river

reservoir

The water is pumped by a pumping station into pipes called water mains. These run into the town beneath the streets to fire hydrants, and to smaller pipes leading to buildings. New York's water mains carry 5,387 million litres a day through 9,000 km of pipes. Most cities pump the treated water to storage tanks on hills or towers. Gravity then creates the pressure needed to push the water through the mains. In London, as much as one-third of all water is lost through old, leaking water mains and pipes.

MAKE A WATER FILTER

Pierce a hole in the lid of a plastic bottle large enough for a straw to fit in securely. With the straw pushed in about 2 cm, screw on the lid. Cut off the bottom of the bottle and secure it in place upside down. Use clamps or tape it firmly between the seats of two chairs.

First pack the neck of the bottle with cotton wool. Then slowly pour in a layer of large-sized gravel, then a layer of small-gravel, then the large-grained sand followed by the fine sand. Cover the top layer with absorbent paper. You have made a water filter.

Stir two spoonfuls of soil into a jar of water. Place a clean empty jar under the straw and slowly pour the muddy water into the filter. How clean is the water that you collect? Repeat this with water with four spoonfuls of soil. Do you have to pour the filtered water through the bottle again to end up with clear water?

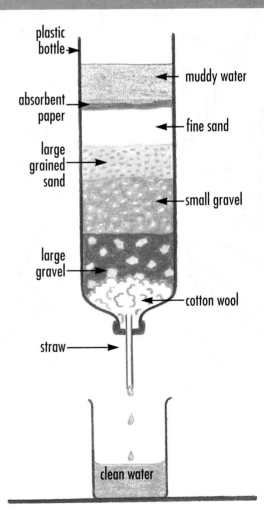

plastic bottle

muddy water

absorbent paper

fine sand

large grained sand

small gravel

large gravel

cotton wool

straw

clean water

Waste and sewage

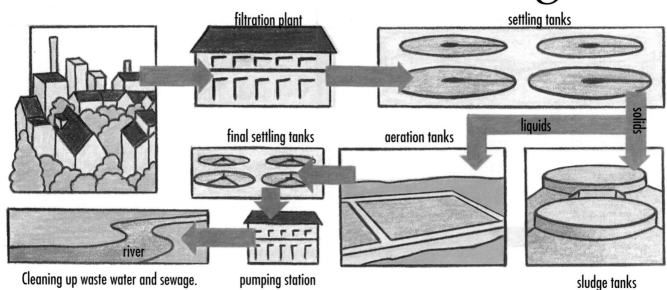

Cleaning up waste water and sewage.

A city is rather like a living thing. It takes in water and food, and gives out waste materials.

In most cities up to 150 years ago, waste water from homes and factories was thrown into gutters or into the river. But a time came when the rivers could no longer cope. In June 1858, the unusually hot weather made the Thames in London smell so appalling that people couldn't approach it without handkerchiefs over their mouths and noses. Traffic on the river stopped as did business in the Houses of Parliament. This was the so-called 'Great Stink'; the result of centuries of careless waste disposal into the river.

New methods of treating sewage before it was poured into rivers were invented in the middle of the nineteenth century – and

have changed little since. But the waste has increased. Underground pipes called sewers carry waste from buildings to the sewage works. First the sewage passes through screens to filter out large objects which are removed for burning. Sewage is pumped through channels where stones sink to the bottom and are removed and washed. These materials are sometimes used to fill holes in roads or building sites.

The remaining sewage passes into tanks where solid material sinks to the bottom – the sludge. The liquid is poured off and sent to tanks where microbes feed on the waste material. It then passes through another tank where the microbes are removed for re-use, and the treated water flows into the river – where natural purification finishes the job.

The sludge is pumped to tanks where over several weeks more microbes work on the waste and turn it into a gas. The sludge is finally removed – some is sold to farms as fertilizers, but some contains chemicals from industry and cannot be used on farmland. It is burned, or sometimes taken to sea in barges and dumped.

A bird's eye view of an English town's sewage works.

Bath or shower?

Do you prefer to shower or bath? A shower uses only around half or one-third of the water of a bath. Test your shower by turning it on to its normal flow and collecting the water in a bucket for 15 seconds. Measure this water and work out how much you use when you have a shower by multiplying this amount by four times the number of minutes you shower for.

Dripping taps

Turn a tap on slightly so that it drips and time how long it takes for half a litre to escape. It could take as little as a minute. Check to see if any taps are dripping and turn them off firmly or get them repaired.

Flushed away

Most of the drinkable water in your home is used to flush the toilet – up to 23 litres per flush! Try putting a plastic bottle filled with water, with the cap on, in the toilet cistern. This will reduce the amount of water used in each flush by about 4 litres. If the toilet is flushed ten times a day – how much water would be saved in a year?

Leaking taps – even one dripping tap could waste 250,000 litres of water a year!

Trash city

The average citizen of an industrial country throws out nine times his or her weight of solid waste a year. Every year, the average US household throws away 1800 plastic items, 13,000 paper things, 500 aluminium cans and 500 glass bottles.

Paper and card are the biggest part of our household waste – most of it is packaging. Paper is made from trees – and each year every person in Britain uses six trees' worth of paper. Drinks cans are made from steel or aluminium – both needed a lot of energy to produce and need raw materials which had to be mined from the land. Each year in the UK about £25 million worth of cans are thrown away.

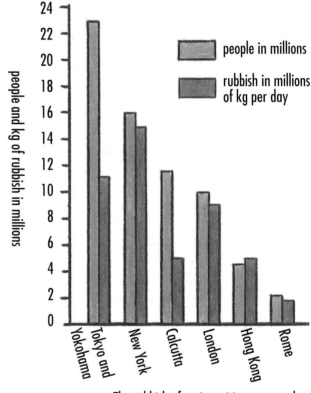

The rubbish of various cities compared.

Young people clearing rubbish from their city – Los Angeles, USA.

Recycling means making new things from old instead of throwing them away. It saves raw materials, energy and the cost of disposing of so much waste.

Bottle and can banks are familiar in most cities. Of the 50 largest US cities, 47 have schemes where people sort their rubbish into separate crates for glass, paper, plastics and cans, and lorries collect the separated rubbish from the kerb.

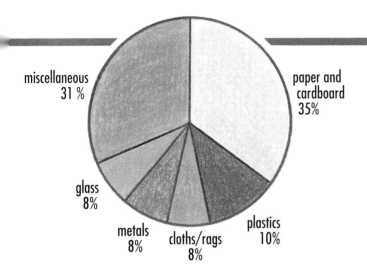

miscellaneous 31%

paper and cardboard 35%

glass 8%

metals 8%

cloths/rags 8%

plastics 10%

What an average North American, Australian or European rubbish bin holds.

In many cities recycling has long been a way of life. Calcutta is India's most densely populated city, creating 3,150 tonnes of solid waste a day. About 70 per cent is collected by the city authority and old cloths and rags are re-used or shredded to fill mattresses or to make rugs. Plastics are melted down and used to manufacture items such as toys. Calcutta's large glass-making industry re-uses waste glass and the waste metal is melted down for re-use by the city's steel industry.

WASTE WATCH

First, ask an adult if it is alright to examine a full waste bin. Wear kitchen gloves and empty the waste on to old newspaper – preferably out of doors! Sort the materials you find into groups such as paper, glass, metal and plastic. Record the number of each item on your chart. Can it be used again or recycled? What was the item used for? Was it necessary? How many items were used as packaging?

Waste material	Items	Number of items	Can it be used again?	Was it necessary?
Paper	newspapers, bags, cereal packets			
Glass				
Wood				
Metal				
Plastic				
Foodstuff				
Other				

To the dump

In most cities there are regular collections of rubbish. It is carted away in lorries for 'disposal'. In the US around 180 million tonnes of solid waste is created each year. Despite laws to improve recycling, this is expected to rise to 250 million tonnes by the year 2010. Just 20 per cent of this rubbish is recycled, 10 per cent is burned and the rest is taken to 'landfill' sites. These are usually holes left by old quarries.

Landfills have to close when full or when polluted water leaks out and affects water supplies. There are 6,600 landfills in the US, but some regions are quickly running out of room to dump and bury their wastes.

In Sweden, Germany and Japan more waste is burned. This reduces the amount of rubbish to be dumped but the ash can contain poisonous chemicals concentrated by the burning. The cost is also greater; it costs $60 a tonne to bury rubbish. Burning costs three times as much.

Scientists in the US have excavated tunnels into the heart of old landfills. They found paper taking up to half of all the space – much of it newspapers and old phone books. Inside the dump everything is squashed and there is little oxygen to decompose things. The scientists found 40-year-old newspapers that could still be read.

Rubbish dumps become mini-cities of their own, teeming with life especially scavengers such as gulls.

It's a rat's life on a rubbish tip.

The rubbish tip is also a home. Gulls are the chief scavengers and many have abandoned a life at sea for the reliable food of the dump. Crows, starlings, house mice and brown rats also feed here. Feasting on the refuse are armies of insects – flies, springtails, as well as woodlice and earthworms. These creatures as well as bacteria and fungi convert the rubbish into fertilizer that will nourish plants. Daisies and dandelions soon grow on a dump, followed by thistles and nettles.

MAKE A WORM COMPOSTER BIN

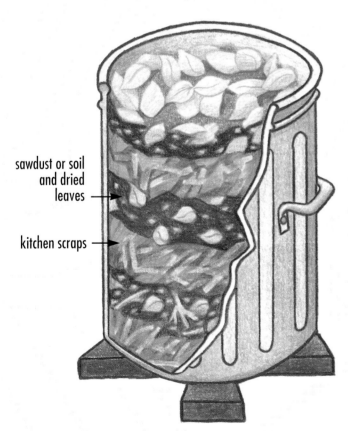

sawdust or soil and dried leaves →

kitchen scraps →

Instead of throwing out your food wastes, why not turn them into compost? You will need an old rubbish bin with a few holes punched into its base.

Place the bin on bricks or blocks of wood so the air can flow underneath and any liquid can drain out. Make sure you have plenty of sawdust or soil and dry leaves and make alternate layers of these dry materials and the kitchen scraps. Use any scraps except fatty foods like meat and cheese. Occasionally add garden clippings to the scraps. From time to time, push a thick stick or broom handle into the mixture to let air reach inside.

When your bin is full you should wait three or four months for compost to be created by the tiny life forms. Now use this plant food in a garden.

Industrial waste

Many industries create waste chemicals which have to be dealt with. Humans have made about 50,000 new chemicals which do not exist in nature, but which have been released into the environment. Few have been fully tested to see what effect they have on living things.

For much of the last 200 years, industries have buried waste acids and metals and other dangerous chemicals leaving no records of what was buried. Years later, houses have been built on these sites. One such place was Love Canal in Niagara City, USA. About 43,000 tonnes of chemicals were buried here and later a school and housing estate were built over the dump. After 20 years the area was tested and the dump was found to be leaking; the air, water and soil were filled with chemicals. About 240 families were moved out of the area, and more families followed later. This was the first time a national emergency had been called in the US because of pollution.

What can be done with dangerous chemicals and polluted soil? Some countries burn this waste – but even at high temperatures new, dangerous chemicals can be made by the burning. The best way to deal with the waste problem is for industries to change

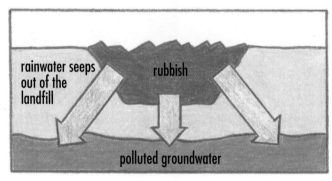

More than 90 per cent of the world's household and dangerous waste is buried in landfills. If the sites have no lining, the chemicals can seep out and pollute groundwater.

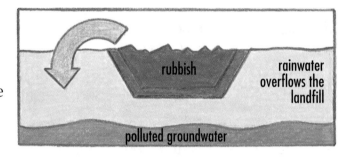

Many countries only bury dangerous waste in landfills lined with clay or plastic to try to stop the chemicals leaking out. But heavy rain can cause the sites to overflow; over time, some chemicals can 'eat away' the lining.

their methods. The 3M Corporation in the USA has redesigned the way it makes its products and re-uses some of the waste material. It has prevented making 16,000 tonnes of water pollutants and 400,000 tonnes of solid waste every year. Although it is expensive for companies to change the way they work, 3M has saved $500 million in materials, energy and disposal costs.

People had to abandon 180 houses on this estate in the UK city of Portsmouth when it was discovered that their homes were built over a chemical dump used 50 years before. There are believed to be 100,000 polluted sites in the UK.

GROWING WATERCRESS

Fill each of six clean bottles with the substances below, and write the number on each. If you make the bleach sample, ask an adult for help. Make five small holes in each of six empty margarine tubs (for drainage) and line each with cotton wool. Number each tub, and add water from bottle 1 to tub 1, from bottle 2 to tub 2, and so on. Sprinkle some cress seeds in each tub and cover with the lids. After three days remove the lids and then add a little of each tub's water every day.

Water them for six days then compare the results. The cress in tub 1 grew normally. Which chemicals had the most effect on the plants? Does water need to be very polluted to have an effect?

Sample number	Liquid used to water the cress	Effect on the cress after 6 days
1	clean tap water	
2	clean tap water plus 1 drop washing up liquid	
3	clean tap water plus 1 pinch of cooking salt	
4	clean tap water plus 1 drop of cycle oil	
5	clean tap water plus 1 drop of house plant food	
6	clean tap water plus 1 drop of bleach	

Towns in balance

A street market in Suzhou, China – a place where most waste food and sewage goes back to fertilize the farms.

Think of the many ways your town or city is like a living thing – like you.

Every day cities eat and drink huge amounts of food, water and energy. These flow through the town rather like food and drink does through a body. Beneath a city's streets, gas, electricity and water flows though pipes rather like the blood vessels of an animal. And waste materials flow out through other pipes or in garbage trucks to be treated and dumped out of the town. A city even draws air into its centre – and is responsible for most of the air pollution created by power stations.

Like any living thing, a town depends on the world outside to survive. The food we buy in supermarkets may have come from the nearby countryside, or a plantation thousands of kilometres away. The electricity we use to watch TV has come from a power station outside the city, using a fuel that was mined on the other side of the country – or the other side of the world.

All that cities usually give back to nature is waste into the air, water and land. Nutrients in farmland, for example, are removed and travel in food to the city. Here they are eaten and end up as sewage.

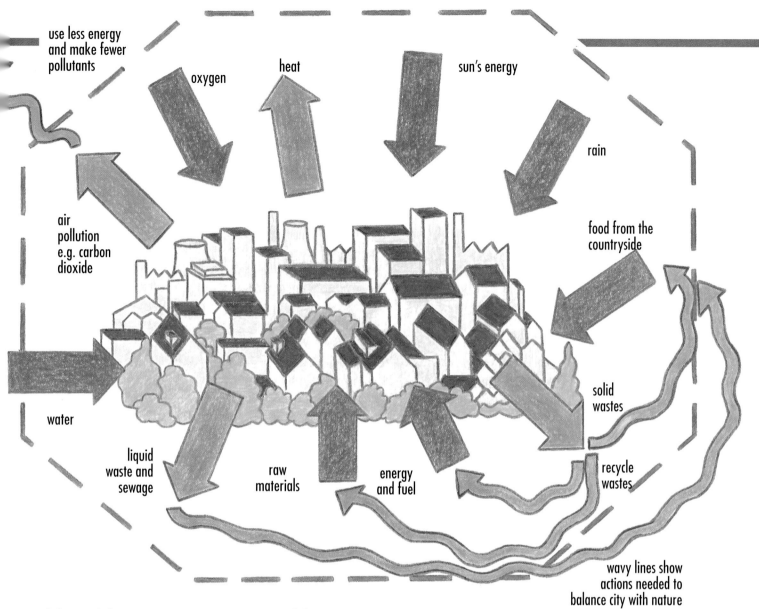

use less energy and make fewer pollutants

oxygen

heat

sun's energy

rain

air pollution e.g. carbon dioxide

food from the countryside

water

solid wastes

liquid waste and sewage

raw materials

energy and fuel

recycle wastes

wavy lines show actions needed to balance city with nature

Most of these nutrients are removed from the land forever. But cities can be made to support themselves. Of China's 15 largest cities, 14 have their own farms around them in the suburbs. These provide most of the cities' food and the sewage is returned to the cities along with composted food wastes.

In wealthier nations, more sewage is now being re-used as fertilizer and less is dumped in the sea or burned. In the same way, many cities now burn much of their

Like a living thing, a town takes in energy and materials from the environment and gives back waste. But the energy and material needs of a city can be reduced; much of the waste can be re-used or recycled.

solid waste and make heat and electricity for themselves. Cities, too, are finding ways of using less electricity, and so reducing air pollution. In this way, cities could become more like true living things – and be in balance with nature.

Glossary

Acid rain Gases released from the burning of fuels such as coal can combine with the water in the air to give acid rain which damages trees, rivers, lakes and buildings.

Adapt To change and adjust to the environment.

Algae A major group of simple plants without stems, roots and leaves.

Bacteria Tiny living things which cause the decay of plant and animal remains and wastes.

Compost A mixture of decaying plant waste which can be used as fertilizer.

Ecology The study of how living things affect each other, and how they are affected by their environment.

Ecosystem The group of animals and plants living in their environment.

Environment Everything, both living and non-living, that surrounds and affects a life form.

Fungi Simple plants that take their food from living or dead plants and animals.

Igneous rock Rock that has formed from once molten material under the Earth's surface.

Industrial Revolution This changed the countries of Europe and North America from nations whose wealth was based on farming into those based on machinery and factories. It began in the eighteenth century.

Larva Some creatures such as insects undergo great changes as they grow from egg to adult. A larva emerges from an egg and sheds its skin several times to allow for growth.

Metamorphic rock Rock created by being changed because of great weight and heat.

Microbes A tiny living thing which can only be seen through a microscope, especially bacteria.

Nutrients Essential substances in soil and water which plants need to produce their food.

Pollution The release of substances into the air, water or land which may upset the natural balance of the environment. Such substances are called pollutants.

Rainforests The dense, evergreen forest found in some of the tropical areas of the world.

Sedimentary rock Rock made by the natural cementing together of tiny particles of sand.

Smog A harmful mixture of moisture, smoke and gases that may form in the air over towns.

Species The name given to the smallest grouping or 'type' of plant and animal. There are believed to be about 30 million different species on the Earth.

Resources

Organizations to contact

United Kingdom
Aluminium Can Recycling
Association, Suite 308
Imex House, 52 Blucher Street
Birmingham B1 1QU

British Effluent and Water
Association, 51 Castle Street
High Wycombe, Bucks HP13 4RN

British Waste Paper Association
Station Road, Aldershot
Hants GU11 1BQ

Centre of the Earth
42 Norman Street, Winson Green
Birmingham B18 7EP

Council for Environmental Education
University of Reading
Reading RG1 5AQ

Friends of the Earth
26-28 Underwood Street
London N1 7JQ

Global Action Plan
42 Kingsway, London WC2B

London Ecology Unit, Bedford House
125 Camden High Street
London NW1 7JR

Tidy Britain Group, The Pier
Wigan WN3 4EX

Trust for Urban Ecology
PO Box 514, London SE16 1AS

Waste Watch, 68 Grafton Way
London W1P 5LE

Australia
Australian Association for
Environmental Education
GPO Box 112, Canberra, ACT 2601

Australian Conservation Foundation
340 Gore Street, Fitzroy, VIC 3065

Friends of the Earth
PO Box 530E, Melbourne, VIC 3001

Canada
Friends of the Earth
251 Laurier Avenue W, Suite 701
Ottawa, Ontario K1P 5J6

International Council for Local
Environmental Initiatives
City Hall, East Tower, 8th Floor
Toronto, Ontario M5H 2N2

Pollution Probe, 12 Madison Avenue
Toronto Ontario, M5R 2S1

New Zealand
Environment and Conservation
Organizations of New Zealand
PO Box 11057, Wellington

Friends of the Earth
PO Box 39-065, Auckland-West

Books to read

Chris Baines, *The Wild Side of Town*,
BBC Books, 1986
Michael Chinery, *Wildlife in Towns and
Cities*, Country Life Books, 1985
Jennifer Cochrane, *Urban Ecology*,
Wayland, 1987
Jennifer Cochrane, *Water Ecology*,
Wayland, 1987
John Corn, *Town and Village Patterns*,
Arnold Wheaton, 1986
The Earth Works Group, *50 Simple
Things Kids Can Do to Save the Earth*,
Sphere, 1990.
Ron Freethy, *Wildlife in Towns*,
Crowood Press, 1986
Barbara James, *Recycling*, Wayland,
1990
Aileen Mackenzie, *City Lights*,
WWF, 1991
Norman Myers (ed), *The Gaia Atlas of
Planet Management*, Gaia, 1994
Philip Neal, *The Urban Scene*,
Dryad, 1987
Philip Parker, *Water for Life*,
Simon & Schuster, 1990
Wildlife on Your Doorstep, Reader's
Digest, 1986
Tony Reynolds, *Cities in Crisis*,
Wayland, 1989
Richard Spurgeon, *Ecology*,
Usborne, 1988
Ron Wilson, *The Urban Dweller's
Wildlife Companion*, Blandford, 1983
WWF/Birmingham DEC, *Where We
Live*, WWF UK, 1989

REFERENCE

Index

Numbers in **bold** refer to an illustration; numbers in *italics* refer to a project or case study.

ailments
   allergies 22
   breathing problems 22
   heart diseases 23
   lung diseases 23
air 4, 20, 21, 22, 42, 44
   chemicals 22, 42
   exhausts 22
   pollution 22, **23**, *23*, 24, 44, 45, 46
   quality *25*
air conditioning 21
airports 28
architecture 10

building materials 4, 6, 8, 12, 26, 28
   asphalt 20
   bricks 8
   clay 8, 28
   concrete 4, 8, **8**, 20
   glass **9**, 10
   granite 8
   gravel 28, 29
   metal 28
   plastic **9**
   sand 8, 28
   steel 10
   stone 8, **8**
   timber 29
   wood 28
buildings 4, **5**, 6, 8, 9, **10**, 11, 21, 28
   castles **5**, 6, **7**
   cathedral **4**, 10, **11**
   church 10, 11
   factories **11**, 12, 21, 36
   houses 12, 42, **42**
   listed 11, **11**
   offices 21
   supermarket **11**, 44
   timber-framed 10

churchyards 12
cities
   heat island 20, **20**, 21
   pollution 22, 24
   suburbs 22, 45
countryside 20, 21

ecology 5, 46
ecosystem 4, 46
electricity 4, 30, **30**, 31, **31**, 44, 45
energy 4, 27, 30, 31, 38, 42, 44
   fossil fuels 30
   hydroelectric power 31
   nuclear 31
environment 4, 5, 42, 46

farms 18, 26, 37, 45
farmland 19, 28, 29, 37, 44
   fertilizers 27, 37
food 4, 6, 26, 27, 36, 44, 45
   bread 27
   eggs **27**
   growing **27**
   intensive farming 27

habitats 12, 14
harbours 6, **6**, 7
heating 21

industry 6, 11, 16, 18, 19, 37, 42
   brickworks 28
   pits 28, 29, **29**
   quarries 28, 40
   raw materials 6, 38
industrial areas 6, 25
Industrial Revolution 7, 14, 46

living things 4, 5, 16, 36, 41, 42, 44, 45
   animals 4, 16, 20, 29, 44
   bacteria 16, 17, 34, 46
   bees 4
   birds 4, 12, **13**, 15, 24

fish 14, **14**, 15, 16, 18
forests 4, 12, 13, 29
insects 12, 25, 41
lichens 24, 25, **25**, *25*
mammals 12, 29
plants 4, 11, 14, 15, 16, 17, 20, 29
rainforests 29
trees 4, **12**, 13 *13*, 15, **21**, 24, **24**, 29, 38
water birds 15, 29, 32
woodland 6, 12, 15

pollution 14, 17, 18, 19, 22, 24, 27, 42, 44, 45, 46
   acid rain **4**, 24, **24**, 31, 46
   chemical 18, 19, 42
   smog 22, 46
   smog alert **22**
power stations 16, **30**, **31**, 32, 44
projects
   air pollution *23*
   air quality *25*
   composter bin *41*
   growing watercress *43*
   look for lichens *25*
   make a water filter *35*
   plant a tree *13*
   river pollution *17, 19*
   waster watch *39*
   water watch *37*

railways 28
rainstorm **21**
rainwater 4, 14, *33*, 34
recycling **5**, 38, 39, 40
reservoirs 12, 29, 32, **32**, 33, 34
rivers 6, 7, 11, 12, 14, **14**, 15, **15**, 16, 17, 18, **18**, 19, **19**, 21, 27, 32, 33, 34, 36
   pollution *17, 19, 19*
   pollution indicator **16-7**
roads 4, 6, 12, 28, **28**, 29

rocks 8, 28, 29
   igneous 8, 46
   marble 9, **9**
   metamorphic 8, 9, 46
   slate 9, **9**
   sedimentary 8, 46
   waterproof 32

Site of Special Scientific Interest 29

Thames Bubbler *19*
towns
   history 6, 11
   industrial 14
   market 6, 26
   names 7
   street names 10
   suburbs 11

waste 4, 5, 19, 20, 36, 38, 44
   chemicals 37, 40, 42, 43
   collection 38, **38**, 40
   compost *41*, 46
   dumping 18, 37, 44, 45
   household 38, **38**, 39,*39*
   landfill 40, **42**
   rubbish **5**, 29, 38, **38**
   rubbish tip **40**, 41, **41**
   sewage 16, 18, 21, 36, 44, 45
   sewage works 36, **36**, 37
water 4, 6, 27, 32, 36, 42, 44
   aqueducts **33**
   boiling 8
   drinking 27, 33, 34, **34-5**
   filter 35, **35**, *35*
   groundwater 42
   leaks 35, **37**
   mains 35
   polluted 16, 17, 40, *43*
   tap 4, **37**
   treatment 34, **34**
   waste 4, 16, **36**, **37**
winds 20, 21